SU_____
Silly
JOKES
for
Kids

© 2020 by Impact Creative Services, LLC, and Happy Fox Books, an imprint of Fox Chapel Publishing Company, Inc., 903 Square Street, Mount Joy, PA 17552.

Super Silly Jokes for Kids is an original work, first published in 2020 by Fox Chapel Publishing Company, Inc. Reproduction of its contents is strictly prohibited without written permission from the rights holder.

ISBN 978-1-64124-067-3

Library of Congress Control Number: 2020935275

To learn more about the other great books from Fox Chapel Publishing, or to find a retailer near you, call toll-free 800-457-9112 or visit us at *www.FoxChapelPublishing.com*.

We are always looking for talented authors. To submit an idea, please send a brief inquiry to acquisitions@foxchapelpublishing.com.

Fox Chapel Publishing makes every effort to use environmentally friendly paper for printing.

Printed in the United States of America
Sixth printing

SUPER Silly JOKES for Kids

VICKI WHITING
ILLUSTRATED BY JEFF SCHINKEL

Happy Fox BOOKS

"Outside of a dog, a book is man's best friend. Inside of a dog, it's too dark to read."

– GROUCHO MARX

Congratulations! You are now holding a book that will bring laughter to your world.

Q: Why did the chicken cross the road?

A: To get a copy of this joke book!

This book has more than 200 jokes designed to make you and your friends and family laugh.

Q: Where do crayons like to ski each winter?

Q: What do you call a 100-year-old ant?

Q: Why did the vampire visit the library?

Stumped? Turn the pages of this book to discover some seriously silly answers!

Laughter brings people together. And a joke that makes people laugh, smile, or even groan brings joy to the world.

Try the jokes out on your friends, family, and teachers as well. They are for anyone who needs a laugh!

Why will a shark avoid eating a clownfish?

They taste funny.

What's the favorite snack of sea monsters?

Fish and ships.

What do whales like to chew?

Blubber gum.

Why are fish such terrible basketball players?

They're afraid to go near the net.

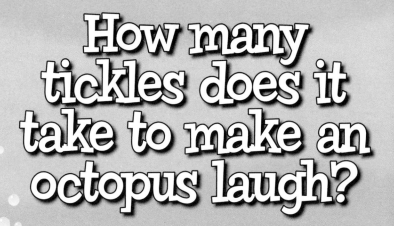

How many tickles does it take to make an octopus laugh?

Ten-tickles.

What is a vampire's favorite fruit?

Neck-tarines.

Why did the zombie stay home from school?

He felt rotten.

What does a ghost do when it gets in a car?

Fastens its sheet belt.

HARRY CLOTTER

Why did the vampire visit the library?

He wanted to sink his teeth into a good book!

8

How do monsters like their coffee?

With scream and sugar.

What kind of fish do pirates like best of all?

Goldfish.

Why don't pirates play cards when they're at sea?

They're usually standing on the deck.

What do you call a pirate who designs buildings?

An ARRRchitect.

What lies at the bottom of the sea and trembles constantly?

A nervous wreck.

What sort of grades did the pirate earn in school?

He had a sea average.

How do fleas travel from place to place?

They itch-hike.

Why did the police officer issue a ticket to the insect?

For being a litterbug.

What do you call a 100-year-old ant?

An antique.

What flies through the air and goes zzub zzub zzub?

A bee flying backwards.

Why don't flies fly through screen doors?

They don't want to strain themselves.

Why do nurses always have red crayons?

In case they need to draw blood.

What did the marble block say to the artist?

"Don't take me for granite."

Where do crayons like to ski each winter?

In Colorado.

What do painters do whenever they get cold?

They put on another coat.

What did the artist tell her boyfriend on Valentine's Day?

"I love you with all my art!"

What did the fog say to the valley?

"I mist you."

Why was it so windy inside the sports arena?

It was full of fans.

What's a tornado's favorite game?

Twister!

What do you get when you leave your teddy bear out in the rain?

A drizzly bear.

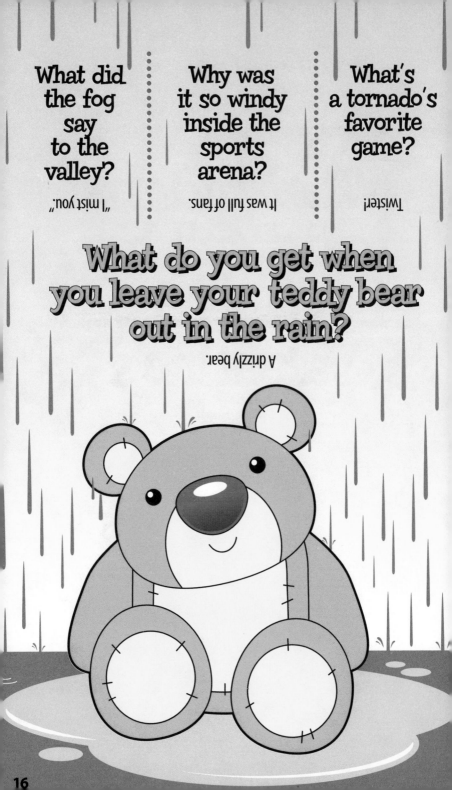

Match each riddle with its punch line.

What do you get when you cross a snowman with a shark?

What do you get when you cross a snowman with a ghost?

What do you call a snowman in June?

Who is a snowman's favorite relative?

What do snowmen eat for breakfast?

Ice screams!

Aunt Arctica!

A puddle!

Frostbite!

Frosted flakes!

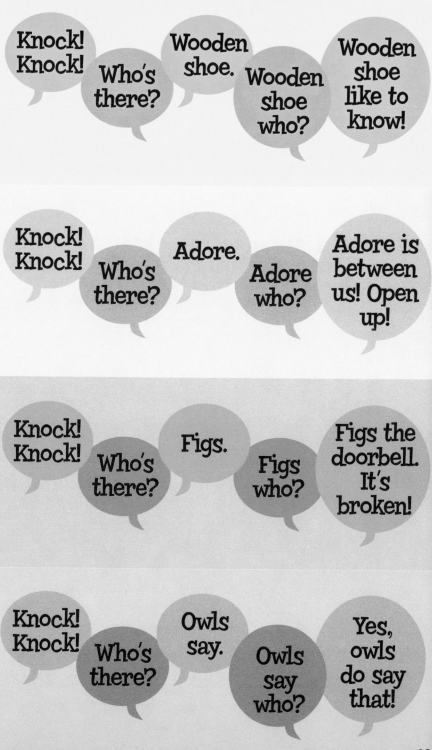

Why did the pine tree get in trouble?

For being knotty.

Did you hear the joke about the oak tree?

It's acorn-y one.

What did the pine trees wear to the lake?

Swimming trunks.

Are mountains really funny?

Yes! They're just hill areas!

What kind of jacket do you wear on a hike?

A trail blazer.

Why did the rooster cross the road?

To show he wasn't chicken.

What do you call a chicken who tells a lot of jokes?

A comedihen.

What do you give a sick bird?

Medical tweetment.

What did the bird say when she found a sweater on sale for just one dollar?

"Cheap! Cheap!"

Why does a flamingo lift up one leg?

Because if it lifted up two legs, it would fall over!

23

Why was the jar of jelly late to work?

What kind of snakes are found on cars?

Which dinosaur is the worst driver?

It got stuck in a traffic jam.

Windshield vipers.

Tyrannosaurus Wrecks.

Who removes old road signs?

A professional de-signer.

Where do cars like to go swimming?

In the carpool lane.

Why is money called dough?

If you want to borrow money, which animal can help you?

Do skunks usually carry a lot of money?

What's the difference between fake dollar bills and an angry rabbit?

When does it rain money?

When there's change in the weather.

Why shouldn't you share jokes about germs?

So you don't spread them around.

When does a doctor get really upset?

When he runs out of patients!

What did the airline pilot do when she got sick?

She flu home.

Why did the bacteria cross the microscope?

To get to the other slide.

Why did the gingerbread cookie visit the doctor?

It was feeling crumb-y.

How do you watch a river on your computer?

Live stream it.

How do you know when you're getting close to a river?

You can hear it creek.

Why is it easy to work with rivers?

They just go with the flow.

What kind of rocks will you never find in the Mississippi River?

Dry ones.

What do you call all of the little rivers that feed into the Nile River?

Juve-niles.

How did the lemon react to losing the race?

Bitterly.

Why was the grapefruit unable to finish the race?

It ran out of juice.

Why did the lime go to the doctor?

It wasn't peeling well.

Why did the orange get thrown out of the frozen juice factory?

Because it wouldn't concentrate.

What's green and smells like orange paint?

Green paint.

How do
robots eat
salsa?

With microchips.

Why was the
robot so
tired after
its commute
home?

It had a hard drive.

What made
the robot
angry?

People kept pushing
its buttons.

How do robots shave?

With a laser blade.

Why did the robot ghost haunt the graveyard?

So it couldn't rust in peace.

Why will you never be hungry in the desert?

Think of all the **sand-which-is** there!

What's the best way to avoid a cold in the summer?

Catch it in the winter.

How do ghosts stay cool in the desert?

With a scare conditioner.

What did one desert cactus say to the other?

"Hey! Long time, no sea!"

What do animals use to hide in the desert?

Camel-flage.

How do farmers count their cattle?

With a **cow**culator.

What did the coach say to the herd of dairy cows?

"Get on the field and give me 2%!"

How do cows keep up with current events?

With the **moos**paper.

Where do cows go for lunch?

The **caf**feteria.

What did the farmer tell the cows when he caught them grazing in the middle of the night?

"It's pasture bedtime!"

How can you tell when your clock is hungry?

It'll go back four seconds.

What do you get when you mix a chicken and a clock?

A duck.

What do you call a belt made of clocks?

A waist of time.

Why was the clock sad when the family left the house each day?

It had no one to tock to.

What did the second hand on the clock say to the hour hand?

"I'll be back in a minute!"

Dinosaurs are excellent at which sport?

Squash.

Which kind of dinosaur performs magic tricks?

A dinosorcerer.

Where does a triceratops sit?

On its tricera-bottom.

What do you call a sleeping dinosaur?

A dinosnore.

42

What dinosaur has the best vocabulary?

Thesaurus.

How do you know there's a dinosaur under your bed?

Your nose touches the ceiling.

How do you ask a dinosaur to lunch?

"Tea, Rex?"

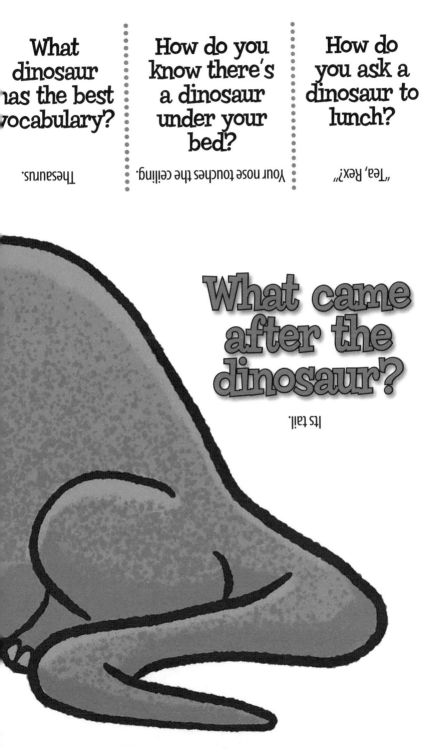

What came after the dinosaur?

Its tail.

Knock! Knock!
Who's there?
Aida.
Aida who?
Aida big lunch today!

Knock! Knock!
Who's there?
Dewey
Dewey who?
Dewey have to wait much longer to get in?

Knock! Knock!
Who's there?
Peas.
Peas who?
Peas open the door!

Knock! Knock!
Who's there?
Dozen
Dozen who?
Dozen anyone want to let me in?

Knock! Knock!
Who's there?
Wool.
Wool who?
Wool you open up?

Knock! Knock!
Who's there?
Theodore
Theodore who?
Theodore wasn't open, so that's why I knocked!

Knock! Knock!
Who's there?
Spell
Spell who?
W-H-O!

Knock! Knock!
Who's there?
Unsharpened pencils.
Unsharpened pencils who?
Never mind. There's just no point.

Knock! Knock!
Who's there?
Alex.
Alex who?
Alex plain when
you open the door!

Knock! Knock!
Who's there?
Two knee fish.
Two knee fish who?
Two knee fish
sandwich!

Knock! Knock!
Who's there?
Iva.
Iva who?
Iva sore hand
from knocking!

Knock! Knock!
Who's there?
Hatch.
Hatch who?
Hey! Please cover
your mouth when
you sneeze!

Knock! Knock!
Who's there?
Needle.
Needle who?
Needle little help
opening the door!

Knock! Knock!
Who's there?
Jester.
Jester who?
Jester minute.
I'll be right back!

Knock! Knock!
Who's there?
Butter.
Butter who?
Butter hurry
and open up!
It's freezing
out here!

Knock! Knock!
Who's there?
Howl
Howl who?
Howl you ever
find out if you
don't open the door?

What do you get when you mix an alien and a kangaroo?

A Mars-supial.

How do you throw a surprise party for an alien?

You have to planet.

What is a space alien's favorite snack?

Rocket chips.

What did the alien say to the garden?

"Take me to your weeder!"

What do you call a spaceship with a bacon pilot?

An Unidentified Frying Object.

What did the elephant do when she hurt her toe?

She called a tow truck.

How do you know when there's an elephant in the refrigerator?

The door won't close.

What's the difference between an elephant and an apple?

The apple is red.

Why did the elephant wear red sneakers?

So it could hide in the strawberry patch.

What do you call an elephant that won't take a bath?

Smellyphant!

Why did the mermaid cross the ocean?

To get to the other tide.

Are mermaids really strong enough to carry a house?

Only if it's a lighthouse.

Why won't clams lend money to mermaids?

Because they're shellfish.

How do mermaids always know exactly how much they weigh?

They bring their scales with them everywhere.

How do mermaids communicate over long distances?

They call each other on their shellphones.

How did the science teacher freshen her breath?

With experi-mints.

Why did the teacher jump into the swimming pool?

He wanted to test the water.

Why did the teacher bring a ladder to school?

She was teaching high school.

Which vegetable do school librarians like best of all?

Quiet peas.

Why did the teacher wear sunglasses in her classroom?

Because her students were very bright.

What does a superhero use to eat her cereal?

What contains chicken broth and noodles and can leap tall buildings?

What did the superhero wear to court?

A superbowl.

Souperman.

His law suit.

Why were the superhero's children the only kids at the playground?

The sign said "SUPERVISION REQUIRED."

Which city has the most superheroes?

Capetown.

Knock! Knock!
  Who's there?
Police.
  Police who?
Police may I come in?

Knock! Knock!
  Who's there?
Ice cream soda.
  Ice cream soda who?
Ice cream soda people can hear me!

Knock! Knock!
  Who's there?
Olive.
  Olive who?
Olive right next door to you.

Knock! Knock!
  Who's there?
Who.
  Who who?
Is there an owl in there?

Knock! Knock!
  Who's there?
Bee two.
  Bee two who?
Bee two school on time.

Knock! Knock!
  Who's there?
Ketchup.
  Ketchup who?
Ketchup with me and I'll tell you.

Knock! Knock!
  Who's there?
Amanda.
  Amanda who?
Amanda repair your doorbell.

Knock! Knock!
  Who's there?
Kenya.
  Kenya who?
Kenya please just open up?

Knock! Knock!
Who's there?
Avenue.
Avenue who?
Avenue answered this door before?

Knock! Knock!
Who's there?
Mustache
Mustache who?
Mustache you some questions.

Knock! Knock!
Who's there?
Witches.
Witches who?
Witches the way back to my house?

Knock! Knock!
Who's there?
Troy.
Troy who?
Troy opening the door and I'll tell you.

Knock! Knock!
Who's there?
Howard.
Howard who?
Howard you like to open this door?

Knock! Knock!
Who's there?
Radio.
Radio who?
Radio not, here I come!

Knock! Knock!
Who's there?
Yukon.
Yukon who?
Yukon open the door and let me in now.

Knock! Knock!
Who's there?
Gladys.
Gladys who?
Gladys almost the weekend.

What does a geometry teacher do in winter?

Makes snow angles.

What do you get by mixing a math teacher and a clock?

Arithmaticks.

What is a math teacher's favorite tree?

Geometree.

Why did the mystery writer use so much graph paper?

Because he was always plotting something.

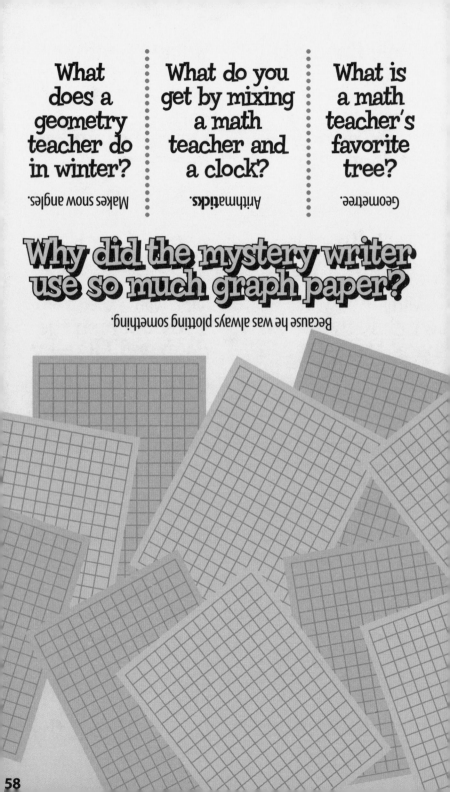

What did one parallel line say to the other parallel line?

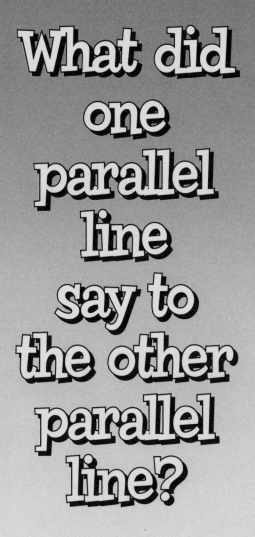

Nothing.
Parallel lines never meet.

Why did the scarecrow skip lunch and dinner?

He was stuffed.

Why was the scarecrow unhappy working in the cornfields?

It was for the birds.

What is a scarecrow's favorite fruit?

Strawberries.

How do you fix a hole in a scarecrow's clothes?

With a pumpkin patch.

Why didn't the kernels leave the popper?

They were cornfused.

What's as big as a cowboy but weighs nothing at all?

His shadow.

How did the cowboy get so rich?

He got a few bucks from his horse every day.

Why do cowboys ride horses?

Because they're too heavy to carry!

Where do cowboys cook their chili?

On the range.

Why did the horse always chew with its mouth open?

It had bad stable manners.

What do frogs wear on their feet?

Open toad sandals.

What shivers, can change colors, and is found at the North Pole?

A lost chameleon.

What kind of food do turtles never eat?

Fast food.

What kind of snakes can you find on a car?

Windshield vipers.

Match each riddle with its punch line.

What can you serve but never eat?

A tennis ball.

Why do ghosts make the best cheerleaders?

They've got spirit, yes they do!

What lights up the soccer stadium?

The match.

Why did Cinderella get kicked off the baseball team?

She kept running away from the ball!

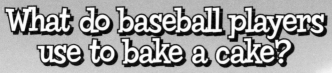

What do baseball players use to bake a cake?

Batter, bunt pans, and oven **mitts.**

Why was the cheese in jail?

It had been up to no gouda.

Why was the grilled cheese sandwich crying?

It was having a total meltdown.

How do you get a mouse to smile for a photo?

Say cheese!

What is a basketball player's favorite kind of cheese?

Swish cheese!

What kind of cheese surrounds a castle?

Moat-zarella.

Why was the math book so unhappy?

It had a lot of problems.

What do you call a kid with a dictionary in his or her pocket?

Smarty pants!

Why was the backpack always sleepy?

It was a napsack.

How many books can you put in an empty backpack?

Just one. After that, it's no longer empty!

Why did the kid throw out his alarm clock?

It kept going off each morning when he was sleeping!

Why doesn't the sun go to college?

It already has millions of degrees!

What did one pig say to the other during the heat wave?

"I'm bacon!"

How can you keep lemons healthy in hot weather?

Give them lemon aid.

What holds the sun up in the sky?

Sunbeams.

What's black and white and red all over?

A panda with a sunburn.

Why did the dinosaur cross the road?

Because chickens weren't around yet!

Why did the biker get a flat tire crossing the road?

Because there was a fork in the road.

Why did the rollerskates cross the road?

The chicken was wearing them!

Why did the chef cross the road with an egg?

She wanted to make it over easy.

Why did the hog cross the road, roll in the mud, and then cross the road again?

It was a dirty double crosser!

What happened to the milk that crossed the road?

It got creamed!

How did the blue bird cross the road?

It jay walked.

What happened to the banana that crossed the road?

It just split.

Why did the cow cross the road?

To get to the udder side.

Why did the fish cross the road?

To get to its school.

Why did the coyote cross the road?

It was chasing the chicken.

Why did the ostrich cross the road?

Because the chicken retired!

What type of markets do dogs try to avoid?

Flea markets.

What kind of kitten is very helpful in an emergency?

A first-aid kit.

Why can't dogs watch movies at home?

They always hit the paws button.

How are dogs and cell phones the same?

They both have collar I.D.

REX